EXCEL AT Group DISCUSSIONS

Your #**1** Guide to Beat the Competition
and Get Ahead at GDs

EXCEL AT Group DISCUSSIONS

Learn to assume key roles, display poise,
enter noisy situations, neutralize arguments, and
many more trenchant tips from a master trainer

DR. PRABAL FRANK

Worldwide Publishing by

Pendown Press

Powered by G Gullybaba

PENDOWN PRESS

Powered by **Gullybaba Publishing House Pvt. Ltd.,**
An ISO 9001 & ISO 14001 Certified Co.,
Regd. Office: 2525/193, 1st Floor, Onkar Nagar-A, Tri Nagar,
Delhi-110035
Ph.: 09350849407, 09312235086
E-mail: info@pendownpress.com
Branch Office: 1A/2A, 20, Hari Sadan, Ansari Road,
Daryaganj, New Delhi-110002
Ph.: 011-45794768
Website: PendownPress.com

First Edition: 2020
Price: ₹259/-
ISBN: 978-93-90479-65-8

Category: Group Discussions, Job Skills, Career Books

The book is sold subject to the condition that it shall not by way of trade or otherwise, be lent, resold, hired out, circulated, and no reproduction in any form, in whole or in part (except for brief quotations in critical articles or reviews) may be made without permission of the author.

Disclaimer: Throughout the book he and she have been used interchangeably. This has been done to avoid the absurdity of English language and not because of any bias towards any sex.

Any advice offered by the author should be used only as a general guideline. It may or may not be suitable for a particular situation. It may differ from person to person, country to country and from time to time. Reader discretion is solicited while applying the strategies given in the book. The author and publisher, individually or corporately, do not accept any responsibility for any liabilities resulting from the actions of any parties involved. Further, the author and the publisher make no claims that using this information will guarantee the reader success in a group discussion.

Layout and Cover Designed by Pendown Graphics Team

Printed and Bound in India by Thomson Press India Ltd.

Illustration Designed by Pendown Illustration Team

DEDICATION

To my father
Mr. Balraj Nandwani
Who inspired me
to write this book.

CONTENTS

Part 3
Popular GD Topics

ABOUT
DR PRABAL FRANK

Prabal is a sought-after after communication and soft-skills trainer by top universities and organizations. He has trained more than 150000 people and served more than 150 organizations in the past 15 plus years. He is an internationally respected expert in the areas of management and communication.

Dr. Frank coaches individuals on communication skills and soft skills to enable them to attain faster career growth and achieve their career dreams. He leads seminars on leadership and allied management aspects for corporate teams to maximize their potential. When not writing, coaching or running seminars, Prabal loves to meditate in solitude.

Some of his clients include: Dabur, Voltas, Godrej, FCI, NAFED, LIC, Punjab National Bank, Axis Bank, Guru Gobind Singh Indrapratha University, Teerthankar Mahaveer University, JIMS University, Lingayas University,

Jamia Milia Islamia, Jamia Hamdard, and K R Mangalam University.

Should you wish to be coached by Prabal, for him to provide a workshop, or speak at a conference then please reach him at drprabalfranknandwani@gmail.com. To know more about him logon to drprabalfranknandwani.com.

To get connected with Prabal on social networks, use the links below:

- Facebook Page: https://www.facebook.com/DrPrabalFrankNandwani
- Twitter Handle: https://twitter.com/DrPrabalFrank
- YouTube Channel: https://www.youtube.com/DrPrabalFrankNandwani

WELCOME

Let me extend you a hearty welcome to the 'Excel at Group Discussions' book. It is a comprehensive guide to beat the competition and get ahead at GDs. I have been engaged in training thousands of students appearing for GDs for SSBs, MBA programs and corporate jobs for the past more than 15 years. In this book, I share with you all that you will need to make sure that you crack the GD with ease and get to you dream course or job.

In this book I will explain why institutes and organisations conduct GDs, how they are constructed and what exactly do evaluators look for in a candidate. You will discover how to act like a pro with excellent insider advice right from how to give the best impression to demonstrating your abilities in a brief time. All this will help you to shine in a GD.

The book has been divided into three parts and it makes sense to go through the book sequentially part-by-part. The first part will enlighten you about the essential questions about a GD like what does it actually mean, how is it conducted and how is your performance evaluated.

In the second part you will learn the various roles which you can adopt to display your skills and leave your competition behind. You will learn how to make a great first impression, how to display what the moderators want to see, and how to stand out from the competition. Furthermore, to ensure your success there are special chapter which make you learn how to win arguments ingeniously and how to deal with difficult situations like someone dominating the GD, your point being pre-empted, etc.

Part three takes you through a list of topics that are generally given in GD to discuss. They have been divided into factual topics, controversial topics and abstract topics.

Whether you're looking to get your favourite course or your dream job, with the assistance of this amazingly simple and effective step-by-step guide you will stand out from the competition, get noticed and crack the GD.

Let's jump right in!

–Prabal Frank

I

PART

UNDERSTAND THE DYNAMICS OF A GD

1. What does a Group Discussion Mean?
2. Why do Organizations Conduct a Group Discussion?
3. How is Performance Evaluated at a GD?

1

WHAT DOES A GD MEAN?

A group discussion (GD) is made of two words and essentially means a bunch of people coming together to discuss about an issue. It is a technique or a method used for screening as well as testing the potential of candidates applying for a job or for admission to a professional course. With the help of a GD it becomes easy to evaluate the comparative strength of the candidates.

In a GD, a group of 10 to 12 candidates is given a topic to discuss among themselves for about 20 to 30 minutes. However, if the number of candidates is less then the GD might just last from 8 to 10 minutes. The performance of the candidates is usually evaluated by a panel of 3 to 4 members.

To collect one's thoughts, 2 to 5 minutes of time is usually given to the participants but there could be instances when this does not happen, so it is best not to rely on this. When the participants have to discuss a case study, however, they are given about 15 minutes of time to study it.

Most organizations and institutes use GD as a selection tool, however, it might be used as elimination tool also. When used as a selection tool, the candidates go through a written test and interview first and finally appear for the GD.

Written Test → Interview → Group Discussion

In fact, now-a-days companies and universities are making GDs their first criteria for screening candidates. This way they are able eliminate more number of people in the very beginning. Subsequently, they will have to spend resources on interviewing only the qualified candidates.

Written Test → Group Discussion → Interview

A person filtering chaff from grain

The Procedure of Conducting a GD

Now since you understand what a GD means the next thing we will discuss is how it is conducted. Well, first the participants are seated around a semi-circular, or circular, or rectangular table. Although, every chair around a circular table offers equal strength in terms of esteem of the occupant, the chairs around a semi-circular or rectangular table offer different esteem levels.

In case of a semi-circular seating, the chair on the non-circular side offers more esteem than others. Similarly, in a rectangular table the chairs in the center offer more weight. These particular chair positions can offer you a natural benefit in terms of being looked upon as a leader, so don't miss the chance to grab them in case there is an opportunity.

Normally you are allowed to carry a piece of paper during the GD for noting down important points but here may be instances when it is proscribed to carry paper.

After getting seated, the participants are given a topic to speak on. The participants do not get equal time to speak. Neither is it mandatory for everyone to speak. However, it is implicit in the concept of a GD to speak. But the participants do not get to distribute the total time available amongst themselves to ensure that everybody gets a fair chance to speak as happens in the case in a debate or elocution. In this sense, a GD is just like a jungle where the one who is fit, or the one who can articulate well, survives.

Although usually the participants are allotted a specific topic to discuss on, however, sometimes it is left to the group to choose a topic for themselves. In such a case, the participants brainstorm and narrow down their options to 3 or 4 before coming to a consensus. In such an eventuality, you should immediately suggest topics which you have a well grounding in as, if chosen, they will give your chances a strong push.

In order to have a more democratic selection of choice, each participant can be asked to rank the 3 most favored topics and the most popular choice should prevail. However, whether it is choosing topics or finding views on particular topic, voting cannot be adopted as a means to arriving at a consensus as a GD is definitely not an election.

Once the discussion has started, sometimes the noise level becomes quite high, more so in cases of controversial topics which has a negative impact on the quality of discussion. In such cases, the moderator might cut short the GD much before the stipulated time. Apart from this where the noise level reaches a high level and in certain other emergency situations, the moderator or the panel members do not intervene in the GD.

Ideally the moderator is supposed to be unbiased and neutral. But realistically it is difficult for any person to be totally free from bias. In case you are acquainted with the moderator you can take advantage by offering arguments which support the facts which the moderator might have a bias for.

At the end, a group is supposed to reach a conclusion. However, usually the time constraints do not allow the group to do so. Some institutes and organizations make the participants write a synopsis of the GD once it is over.

This is the process of a group discussion. By now you have an overview about what happens in a group discussion. Next, we are going to explore what are the various topics which generally the participants are supposed to discuss.

What are the participants supposed to discuss?

The participants of a GD are either given a topic or a case study to discuss. Topic based GDs can be classified into 3 types:

Factual Topics: They are about practical things, which an ordinary person should be aware of in his day-to-day life. Typically these are about socio-economic issues. These can be current, i.e., they may have been in the news lately, or could be unbound by time. A factual topic for discussion gives a candidate a chance to prove that he is aware of and sensitive to his environment. For example:

- The education policy of our country
- State of the aged in the nation
- Tourism in our country

Controversial Topics

They are the ones that the argumentative in nature. They are meant to generate controversy. In GDs where these topics are given for discussion, the noise level is usually high, there may be tempers flying. The idea behind giving a topic like this is to see how much maturity the candidate is displaying by keeping his temper in check, by rationally and logically arguing his point of view without getting personal and emotional. For example:

- Reservations should be removed
- Women make better managers
- Freedom is a myth

Abstract Topics

They are about intangible things. These topics are not given often for discussion, but their possibility cannot be ruled out. These topics test your lateral thinking and creativity. For example:

- Z is an alphabet
- Twinkle twinkle little star
- The number 13

Case Studies

Another variation is the use of a case instead of a topic. The case study tries to simulate a real-life situation. Information about the situation will be given to you and you would be asked as a group to resolve the situation. In a case study there are no incorrect answers or perfect solutions. The objective in the case study is to get you to think about the situation from various angles.

The case study may be technical or non-technical in nature and focuses more on problem-solving and creative skills of the participants.

2

WHY DO ORGANIZATIONS CONDUCT A GD?

People study alone but work in a team. Teams create synergy. Together each one achieves more. One plus one becomes three. The reason why organizations and universities put you through a GD and an interview, after testing your technical and conceptual skills in an exam, is to get to know you as a person and gauge how well you will fit-in. They are able to gauge whether the candidate has certain personality traits and skills that it desires in its team members or students.

Arriving at Collective Decisions

One of the most important daily activities of any business is to take decisions. The world of decision making has changed. Leadership style has moved from being autocratic in the ancient times to being democratic in the contemporary times. Consensus is the key word now. Autocratic style is ancient.

In order to arrive at an educated decision, meetings are conducted. It helps to pool in the knowledge base, experience and creativity of the team members. Brainstorming helps churn the minds of the members and let ideas emerge.

Taking decisions collectively also absolves one particular leader of individual responsibility. Senior management of reputed companies meet regularly to come to a consensus and take important decisions collectively. Even when moving against another country, USA first presents its case in the UN to gain consensus from eminent member countries before moving ahead.

News channels had become views channel long back. Of late they recognized that to prevent polarization of viewers and being labeled as a prejudiced channel it is important to offer a variety of views regarding a story. It also helps the viewers to understand a story from various angles. In the past five years, there has been a trend to have group discussions on burning issues every night at prime time on top TV news channels.

Looking towards the importance of collective decision making in today's environment, the entrance procedure for professional courses like MBA, SSB, etc. as well as the recruitment process for corporate jobs now include getting through a GD as a mandatory requirement.

As a team member or a team leader, you will be required to attend and conduct innumerable meetings. A GD is a simulation of what you can expect in a meeting at your workplace.

Void in the Interview Process

An interview is one-on-one process while a GD is many-on-many process. Normally organizations and universities would go in for an Interview. In an interview, the candidate is expected to respond to questions from either a single interviewer or from the panel of interviewers. However, there are certain qualities of candidates which can be most clearly revealed only in a GD as against other forms of testing.

Unlike in an interview where the participant does get necessarily get a chance to speak, in a GD you to make your chances. You do not get a chance to speak automatically and remaining silent butchers your chances. (How can you brighten up your chances at a GD is discussed in the next part.)

More importantly, what you think about yourself, proclaim in your résumé, or assert in an interview is put to test in a GD. For example, you might mention in your profile that you are excellent at presentation and negotiations. However, self-beliefs might be faulty.

Often times self-beliefs are based on the feedback we get from our environment and our close circle of friends. Khalil Gibran has a wonderful story about a sheep. The story says that a sheep got up in the morning when the Sun has just risen and talked about her desire to have an elephant in lunch that day. However, as the day progressed and Sun came overhead, it said that she had a change of plans and a mouse would be suffice in lunch. Actually, it was the feedback sheep received from her giant-sized shadow in the morning that led her to believe that she was capable to eat a whole elephant. But when the shadow shrunk enormously by noon, as the Sun as overhead, it had to recalibrate and change her plans.

Such a faulty self-evaluation is also witnessed in many singing reality shows on the TV where contestants considering themselves to be virtuosos at singing fall flat in front of the judges. Many of them find hard to believe that their singing which is extolled by their friends has failed to impress the judges. Perhaps the English proverb, 'In the land of the blind, one-eyed man is the king,' says it all. May be that their skills are superior to those around them, however, that does not mean that they quality the benchmark for a good singer.

Your claims to be good at some aspects of communication, interpersonal skills and attitude are tested first hand in a GD, which are not so easy to evaluate in an interview.

Discussion if Different

A GD is nothing but discussion in small groups. So we need to know two things. First, why do organizations need you to be in a group as against other forms of testing where you are required to answer alone? And the second, why do organizations need you to 'discuss' an issue as against 'answering' questions?

In the real world, most positions would require you to work with other people in teams. An individual might be able to perform well while working alone but may prove to be a failure as part of a team. In the latter case, he would become a liability for the organization employing him. The GD tests how you function as a part of a team.

As a part of an organization, you will mostly be working in teams, either as a members or as a leader. Your ability to deal with and manage people would prove vital for your performance Leaders need to work in teams and get best results through teamwork. That is precisely the reason why various organizations and management institutes include GD as a component of the selection procedure. The GD checks your ability to behave, participate and contribute in a group.

Further, by conducting a GD, the organizations need participants to discuss on some issues. What purpose does discussing solve which debating; answering to questions or public speaking does not? Well, there is a considerable difference them. In public speaking, the listeners merely judge but do not compete with the speaker. In GD, however, the listeners have equal right to speak.

Many times participants mix up discussion with a debate. In a debate the focus is on winning but in GD the participants shoot for convincing and want to reach a consensus. Discussion is based more on co-operation while debate is based more on competition. In a discussion, the participants present their points in a logical and methodical manner rather than forcing their point of view on others. A debate, on the other hand, starts with opposite groups' arguments to outwit one another. As the discussion evolves, the participants refine their views in light of the facts which have been put forth by the other participants. Thus, the difference lies both in the style of participation as well as the mental makeup that is needed to successfully participate in either.

Similarly, in an interview, a candidate has to respond to the well directed questions asked by the interviewer. He is given ample opportunities to offer an explanation as the interviewer is interested in his answers. A GD is also different from a debate or a lecture in the sense that the speaker is not given much time to collect and organize his ideas by the person who is chairing the session.

A discussion provides an opportunity to the interviewer to gauge key skills and personality traits of the candidates such as: how much importance do they give to the group objective and their own, how well are they able to express their ideas in a convincing way, how do they take the criticism thrown at them especially by people they don't know much, how open-minded they are in accepting views which are contrary to their own etc. This leads to the physical verification of abstract qualities.

Team leaders need to discuss their way out and not dictate terms to their teams. Moreover, it is through discussions, ideas can be generated which may lead to creative solutions to existing problems. So the ability to discuss successfully is crucial.

Now you understand why it is important for the organizations to conduct a GD. Next we will see how your performance is measured at a GD.

3

HOW IS PERFORMANCE EVALUATED AT A GROUP DISCUSSION?

Your performance at the GD is evaluated on the basis of your participation that is what you said and did during the GD. The essential aspects which make up a GD are verbal communication, non-verbal behavior, conformation to norms, decision-making ability and cooperation. In short the GD gauges the following in a participant:

- Ability to work in a team, assertiveness, ability to handle people
- Leadership skills, initiative

- Attitude, flexibility
- Communication skills, listening skills
- Reasoning ability, creativity, ability to think on one's feet

The above factors can be divided into three broad categories skills, awareness, and traits and are the indices of your performance at a GD. Let us take them up one by one.

Skills

The key skills which the moderators are looking out for to evaluate your performance are:

Communication Skills

These not only include your verbal communication skills like fluency, vocabulary and grammar but also the non-verbal communication like your gestures and postures. It has been witnessed many times that candidates complain about not getting selected even after contributing key ideas during the discussion while the one who is selected merely rehashed the information and got in. Perhaps they are the one who lag behind in communication skills. The participants should not only speak their points but speak in a manner which catches the attention of listeners. Presentation skills in such a situation are paramount. Even the dress which one wears communicates subtly about the person wearing it.

Inter-personal Skills

Since one has to work in a team it becomes essential that she wins the support of the people around her. One should know how to reach out to other team members and how to disagree politely. One has to be good at giving and taking criticism, and have the ability to start conversations conveniently.

Leadership Skills

Leadership is less about dictating and controlling but more about giving direction and taking them together to achieve the goal. It is not about setting the rules but about winning the heart of people so that they are ready to give their best and achieve the organizational goals. Two of the key skills which leaders need to possess are initiative and the ability to persuade and motivate the members.

Thinking Skills

In real life one does not always face problems which he had prepared for while graduating. Life throws unexpected problems and when such an unstructured problem arises, one cannot run away and say that he has not been trained to face such a problem. Thinking skills encompass your creativity and problem-solving ability. They test you on what you will do when you do not have an idea about the problem at hand.

Awareness

The next thing which counts big time during GDs is one's awareness about the environment in which she is living. One does not live in a vacuum. People are dependent on each other and on nature. Things which happen in China do affect the people who live in USA and vice versa. People in North Korea will suffer from polluted water as much as the people in Japan.

The factual topics of a GD are generally based on current issues being faced by the society and test an individual on his awareness about them. They might be related to the earth like the growing pollution levels causing a change in the climate or they might be restricted to the geographical area in which you live like moving the factory outside the city limits.

Traits

The third aspect on which one's performance is evaluated in a GD is her attitude. Things that are gauged can vary right from whether she is dominating, aggressive, assertive, or passive; is she open and amenable to new and convincing ideas or is she the kind of a 'I am right and you are wrong' person; is she honest and admits her mistakes or does she refuse to acknowledge her mistakes; etc.

We take up these key aspects on which one's performance is evaluated in a GD one-by-one at length in the next part. Keep reading!

II
PART

ENGAGING IN A GD

4

START WITH A BANG

GD is also known as a leaderless discussion. It aims to find out the natural leadership level of the candidates. Strictly speaking, no one from the group or outside is officially designated as leader or president or chairman or anything of that sort. Even the examiner or supervisor who launches the discussion returns to the background. No one other than the GD participants intervene in the deliberations of the group.

The participants also do not elect or decide one among them to be their leader. Leadership in a GD is established implicitly through one's performance in the discussion. The best way to participate in a GD is to initiate the discussion. The person who initiates takes the role of a leader mostly.

You can demonstrate leadership ability by:

- Initiating the discussion
- Addressing yourself to the group not to a single individual
- Introducing yourself very precisely in the first two minutes
- Declaring your stand in your very first entry
- Encouraging reticent members to speak
- Summarizing views of others before presenting your own
- Conceding to others view points when they are reasonable

Initiating the Discussion

Initiating a GD is a high risk high reward strategy. When you initiate a GD, you not only grab the opportunity to speak, you also grab the attention of the examiner and your fellow candidates. If you can make a few favorable first impressions with your content and communication skills after you initiate a GD it will help you sail through the discussion. But if you initiate a GD and stammer, stutter or quote wrong facts and figures, the damage might be irreversible.

Moreover, if you initiate a GD impeccably but do not speak much after that, it gives the impression that you started the GD for the sake of starting it or getting those initial kitty of points earmarked for an initiator!

When you start a GD, you are responsible for putting it into the right perspective and framework. So initiate only if you have in-depth knowledge about the topic at hand.

Different techniques to initiate a GD and make a good impression:

Definition

Start a GD by defining the topic or an important term in the topic. For example, if the topic of the GD is 'Advertising is a Diplomatic Way of Telling a Lie,' you can start by defining advertising as, 'Any paid form of non-personal presentation and promotion of ideas, goods or services through mass media like newspapers, magazines, television or radio by an identified sponsor'.

Question

Asking a question is a high impact way of starting a GD. It does not signify asking a question to any of the candidates in a GD so as to hamper the flow. It implies asking a question, and answering it yourself. Any question that might hamper the flow of a GD or insult a participant or play devil's advocate must be discouraged. Questions that promote a flow of ideas are always appreciated. For a topic like, 'Should India go to war with Pakistan,' you could start by asking, 'What does war bring to the people of a nation? We have had four clashed with Pakistan. The pertinent question is what have we achieved?'

Shock Statement

Initiating a GD with a shocking statement is the best way to grab immediate attention and put forth your point. If a GD topic is, 'The Impact of Pollution on the Indian Economy,' you could start with, 'At the center of the Indian capital stands a population clock that ticks away relentlessly. It tracks 33 births a minute, 2000 an hour, 48000 a day. This calculates to about a million every year. That is roughly the size of Australia. As a current poster slogan puts it, 'Nothing is impossible when one billion Indians work together.'

Quotes

For a GD topic like, Customer is King, you could quote Sam Walton's famous saying, 'There is only one boss—the customer. And he can fire everybody in the company from the chairman on down, simply by spending his money somewhere else.'

Facts, Figures and Statistics

If you decide to initiate your GD with facts, figures and statistics make sure to quote them accurately. Approximation is allowed in macro level figures, but micro level figures need to be correct and accurate. For example, you can say, approximately 70 per cent of the Indian population stays in rural areas (macro figures, approximation allowed). But you cannot say 30 states of India instead of 28 (micro figures, no approximations). Stating wrong facts works to your disadvantage. However, an error margin of 5% is acceptable.

Short Story

Use a short story in a GD topic like 'Attitude is Everything.' This can be initiated with, 'A child once asked a balloon vendor who was selling gas-filled balloons, whether a blue-colored balloon will go as high in the sky as a green-colored balloon. The balloon vendor told the child, it is not the color of the balloon but what is inside it that makes it go high.'

General Statement:

Use a general statement to put the GD in proper perspective. For example if the topic is, 'Should Rahul Gandhi be the prime minister of India,' you could start by saying, 'Before jumping to conclusions like, he should be the prime minister or he should not be the prime minister, let's first discuss about the qualities that a person must possess to become the prime minster. Then we can compare these qualities with those that Mr. Gandhi possesses. This will help us reach at a more object decision and in an effective manner.'

Encouraging Reticent Members to Speak

If you openly request someone to speak, you may be putting the other person in a difficult spot, and the evaluators will not look that upon favorably. Do not directly put someone who is consistently silent on the spot by asking him or her to speak up.

If someone has been trying to speak and has a good point but is cut off constantly you may encourage him or her to continue with her point as you would like to hear her out. Use other means of motivation, such as agreeing with a halting speaker, adding on to their points, implicitly supporting and giving them direction.

Summarizing

If the moderator asks you to summarize a GD, it means the GD has come to an end. Most GDs do not really have any conclusions. A conclusion is where the whole group decides in favor or against the topic. But every GD is summarized. You can summarize what the group has discussed in the GD in a nutshell.

Keep the following points in mind while summarizing a discussion:

- Avoid raising new points
- Avoid stating only your viewpoint
- Avoid dwelling only on one aspect of the GD
- Keep it brief and concise
- It must incorporate all the important points that came out during the GD
- Do not add anything once the GD has been summarized

The above strategies are the best to adopt during a GD. They display loud and clear that you have leadership skills and put you in the limelight. However, if someone else initiates the GD before you could, or if you don't know more about the topic of discussion, do not lose heart. There are still a lot of things that you can do and get selected in a GD. This is what we discuss in the next chapter. Read on.

5

ADOPT A TASK ROLE

Your aim at a GD is to get noticed. You should gain a chance to speak, make sure that you speak sensibly and create an impact on the group as well as the evaluators. Also, it must be clearly visible to the evaluators that you are attempting to build a consensus. But to do all this you have to start to participate in the GD.

There are many ways to participate in a GD. Although the best way is to initiate the GD, however, it is not always possible. Besides, only one of the participants can do it, and if it has been done by someone else, perhaps someone more tactful then you have lost that opportunity. But you don't have to fret over it as there are la lot of other roles which the participants can take up in a GD. Moreover, all the stages of a GD are equally important which include the beginning where you initiate, the middle where you elucidate and the end where you conclude.

You can furnish more information by usurping his place. You can politely interfere giving evidence, opinions and relate experiences relevant to the discussion. In fact the quality of the discussion is dependent on the information generated out of the discussion. The more information you provide on the subject the more prominent your place will become in the group.

Okay, you missed this opportunity too. A vociferous participant has stolen the show. All have nothing to do except to listen. The best way is to play the role of an information seeker thereby making your participation important. By way of asking information from others and seeking clarification one can make his participation felt.

There are various ways to make your presence important. Instead of just presenting information one can strongly present his own point of view. Usually people will reveal their opinions out of fear of criticism. But an effective presenter expresses his opinions freely and is prepared to invite argument to his side. By stating out his beliefs, attitudes and judgments, one can take up a main position in the discussion. But you must ensure that your opinion is on the winning side and there is nothing negative in your opinion because a negative opinion is disliked by others.

If you cannot make up your position still there is a role left for you. You can prevail upon the opinion of others. The effective participant actively seeks other's attitudes and convictions, especially of those members who are hesitant to speak. Unlike others who are content with presenting their own views and neglecting other opinion you will win the favor of other participants by seeking their opinions.

There is always room for participation if you elaborate the ideas of others presented before as well as expand on opinions of others through relevant examples and explanations. This is the best way to attract the attention of the rest.

Slow and steady, you can win the race. If you have not yet got an opportunity, take up the role of integrator who classifies the relationships between various facts, opinions and suggestions and integrates the ideas of others thereby assuming the main role of presenter. After a considerable time has been spent on discussion, the need for integrating and summarizing all that transpired so far becomes essential. You can do that by the way of orientation, that is, by keeping the group directed toward its goal, by summarizing what has taken place and clarifying the purpose or position of the group. Essentially you ensure that the group has a direction and also that it heads in the right direction and assume the role of a leader.

There are some more ways in which the participants can take up group maintenance. You should make your presence important by initiating the group's interpersonal relationships. An encouraging speaker is always liked by fellow participants. He praises and agrees with others providing a warm support to others. But one ought to be careful because he who is a contestant should maintain his position keeping his attention on excelling others.

Similarly your sense will be appreciated if it relieves tension. It will be very much appreciated as you create a relaxed atmosphere by reducing formality and interjecting humor. When tension increases, people become emotionally involved which will not be conducive for smooth discussion. At times the role of pacifying others and providing relief will achieve leadership position. Equally important is the role of one who controls the channel of communication providing proper balance in the amount of participation of each member. You can also gain the leading position by encouraging those who might otherwise not speak while tackling those who try to dominate over others or polarize the discussion.

Positive Task Roles to be Adopted

- Initiator
- Information Seeker
- Information Giver
- Opinion Seeker
- Opinion Giver
- Clarifier
- Social Supporter
- Harmonizer
- Tension Reliever
- Energizer
- Compromiser
- Gatekeeper
- Summarizer

Negative Task Roles to be Avoided

- Disgruntled non-participant
- Attacker
- Dominator
- Patronizer
- Clown

6

COMMUNICATE @100%

Communication skills are the most important skills for success at a GD. Every position in the corporate world does not require leadership but all positions do require communication skills. Even your silence shouts about you. Be careful about your words, tone, body language and dress.

In a 20 minute GD with 10 to 12 participants, you should try and participate at least 4 times with each entry lasting at least 25 to 30 seconds. You could participate more depending on your comfort level and the need for participation.

Speaking Skills

> "To speak is one thing, but to
> speak well is quite another."
>
> –Dr. Prabal Frank

Speak Clearly

Those who listen to you will need to understand what you are saying. This could be a major problem for someone who is speaking a language that is not their native tongue. Speak in a manner that will allow the other members to understand exactly what you are saying. Give emphasis on key words in your speech. Also, do not underestimate the power of pauses. You should not need to repeat yourself to make yourself clear to the other participants.

Be Concise

Because most group discussions are restricted to time, it will become tedious to bother you and the other members if you have to repeat what you are saying because they do not understand you. Do not repeat and use irrelevant materials. Do not speak just to increase your speaking time. Your thoughts should be sensible rather than being irrelevant. Also, there is no need to go into too many details. Just a basic subject analysis is sufficient. No need to mention exact figures while giving any reference.

Speak Audibly

Everyone should be able to hear what you are saying. If someone has to ask you to speak up, you will be forced to repeat yourself, and this will waste time. If someone makes a statement that you do not understand, ask them to clarify in a polite manner.

Use Proper Tone

During GDs, it isn't just enough to speak eloquently. It is also important to make sure you speak in a proper tone. If you speak in a harsh manner, you can send across the wrong message to others who are participating in the discussion. This could lead to conflicts, and it is important to avoid this. The tone of your voice and the way you speak will say a lot about how you feel about a certain topic, and it will also show how well you can speak.

Address Correctly

Don't ever make the mistake of addressing the panel members. The GD is between you and the other participants, not the panel members. You must avoid even looking at the panel members while the GD is in progress. Just ignore their existence.

Communicate with each and every candidate present. While you speak don't keep looking at a single member. Address the entire group in such a way that everyone feels you are speaking to him or her.

If you are initiating the discussion, you could do so by collectively addressing the group as 'Friends'. Subsequently, you could use names (if the group has had a round of self-introduction prior to starting the discussion and you remember the names) or simply use pronouns like 'he' or 'she'.

Avoid Technical Terms

Avoid using technical terms. It is quite likely that other participants of the group have a different academic background from you so in case you use some technical terms, do explain its meaning to the other participants. Also refrain from using abbreviations of the technical terms, use full forms instead.

Don't Switch Language

In most of the cases the GD would take place in English. While you discuss don't switch to your native language. Just stick with English.

Use Correct Pronunciation

Although pronunciation varies a little from place to place, yet there are pronunciations which are grossly incorrect. Kindly use the standard pronunciation given in the dictionaries. You might not get more marks if you pronounce correctly but you definitely will end up losing some in case you use wrong pronunciations. Also do not make grammar mistakes while forming sentences.

Use Humor Cautiously

Should I use humor or not? This question looms large on the mind of participants of a GD. Well, the answer is that it depends on the situation. While the noise level is less and the participants are relaxed, it may be acceptable. But in a competitive situation, where the participants are tensed up, your attempts at humor may fall flat.

Absolute Don'ts

- Do not lose your temper. A discussion is not an argument.
- Do not shout. Use a moderate tone and medium pitch.
- Do not dominate the discussion. Confident speakers should allow quieter students a chance to contribute.
- Do not attack any public figure.

Listening Skills

You would not be looked upon favorably if you kept speaking all the time and did not listen to anyone else. Contrary to the misconception, the person who talks the most is not necessarily the one who is judged the best. The quality and not the quantity of your contribution is the success factor.

Make sure that you listen to the names and figures carefully so that you can mention them when you speak next.

It is not only important to listen. It is also important to show that you have been listening. While listening keep nodding your head in frequent intervals to reassure the speaker that he is being listened to.

Non-Verbal Communication

Match with Words

Physical movements should be appropriate to what is said. There should not be any mismatch between what is being said (words) and what is being conveyed (body language).

Moderate Gestures

Don't use too many gestures when you speak. You are discussing not teaching. Further, gestures like pointing finger and table thumbing can appear aggressive.

Maintain Eye Contact

Eye contact plays a major role to form a rapport with the other participants. Imagine how you will feel if someone is talking to you and looking at someone else. So think as if you are playing badminton and never let your eyes off the shuttle. Next, be like a lighthouse which spreads light in all the directions by making eye contact with all the participants in the group rather than just a few of them.

A Badminton player looking at a girl and missing the shuttle

Keep Feet in Control: Keep your feet shoulder distance apart and do not start to produce music with them.

Move Purposely: When you wish to make an important point incline forward towards the participants and when you want to reflect about something important they just said, move backwards. If you wish to change the subject or change the tempo of what you are saying just move sideways either towards your left or right. This way you will be able to manage your impression on people observing you.

Absolute Don'ts

- Do not make faces.
- Do not make music with your hands or feet.
- Do not slouch in a chair.
- Do not keep your legs in a figure four position.

Art of Explanation

Saying and explaining are two different words and have different meaning. Use examples to explain a point. It helps others to understand your idea better but remember to keep it short.

Don't draw too much on personal experience or anecdote as you don't want to generalize too much.

Conversation Etiquette

Interrupt Politely

It is not a good idea to interrupt someone to make your point. If you need to interrupt someone who is peaking, it is always important to interject their conversation in a nice way. Some groups may require you to raise your hand and be called upon before you can comment on a statement or idea. However, if you do have to interrupt here are some acceptable ways of doing it:

- Excuse me, but I feel that what you are saying isn't universally true.

- Yes, I agree with your idea, and I would like to add on to it.

- Yes, I think you are right when you say that, but could you clarify what if...

Avoid Slangs: It is best to avoid using slang during a GD.

Disagree Tactfully

If you disagree with a statement that has been made, do it in a manner that is tactful. Always talk in a manner that is courteous to others. You should not ridicule or attack someone personally because you don't like their idea.

A GD is not a debating stage. Participants should confine themselves to expressing their viewpoints. In the second part of the discussion candidates can exercise their choice in agreeing, disagreeing or remaining neutral.

How did you appear to be?

Candidates are both watched and listened to. Those who keep on shifting stances, fidget with their hands and legs, look towards the panelists for assurance and seek advice from the heavens by looking up are they one's who wind up their chances at clearing the GD. On the other hand, candidates who display patience and could effectively express themselves to the group members while being cooperative and considerate end up cracking the GD.

7

BEHAVE AT YOUR BEST

The golden principle for hiring workforce is 'Hire for attitude and train for skills.' This is based on the understanding that if we have a person with a bad attitude even if he is good at technical skills he will prove harmful for the organization. On the contrary, if someone is good at attitude he can be trained to perform better.

The above principle works in most situations except in positions where we need high level of expertise. And even then if one have an option to take in person with a nice attitude it is better.

Attitude is reflected in behavior of a person and is a key for success. If you are a parent how do you react if your child does not brush after eating chocolate at night. One way is that you just tell him once and if he does not follow you just ignore the subsequent times and go to sleep. This is an example of passive behavior. The other way could have been that you get angry and given him a reprimand and place checks to find out if the child has brushed his teeth. This is an example of dominant behavior.

Apart from a passive and dominant behavior, there is another way to handle such situations. A child can be made to understand that brushing teeth before going to bed especially after having chocolate is important to prevent cavities and you feel emotionally upset if they won't brush their teeth. And still if the child does not listen then you continue with your advice every time he or she eats the chocolate at night and do not just give up on it. This is called assertive behavior.

When there are many people in a team, there are bound to be difference of opinion on what to do and how to do it. In a GD, the moderator wants to gauge your behavior to find out how will you react if you find something that according to you should not be happening. For example, if you find out that your colleague is taking alcohol during office hours how will you react.

The following difference in the personality traits of people will help you understand the difference between aggressive, passive and assertive behaviors:

Belief System

An aggressive person believes that everyone should be like him because he is always right. Moreover he thinks that he has the prerogative but not others. A passive person on the other hand won't express his feelings freely and therefore will not disagree with others. He often feels that others have more rights than he does. An assertive individual believes that he can be right at times and others can be too. He believes in a level playing field where both parties have a right to express themselves and take collective decision.

Characteristics

An aggressive person is very dominating and bullying. He displays a patronizing and criticizing behavior. He achieves goals but at the cost of others; dominating and bullying; patronizing condemning and sarcastic. A passive individual however, is apologetic, self conscious; trusts others more than self and as a natural consequence allows others to take decision for self. He doesn't get what he wants and is readily loses for others. An assertive individual however is not judgmental but confident, open and flexible. He has a sense of humor, and is proactive.

Communication Skills

A person with aggressive attitude is a poor listener, has a closed mind, and does not accept other's views. He displays interrupting and monopolizing behavior. A passive person on the contrary is hesitant and mostly agrees. A person who is assertive listens actively, places his expectation within limits and expressive his thoughts freely.

Behavior

Aggressive person puts others down, never thinks they could be right, and is bossy. A passive person is just the opposite. He sighs a lot, tries to sit on both sides of the fence, asks permission unnecessarily, and lets others make choices even for him. Such a person faces difficulty in implementing plans. An assertive person acts according to a plan. Their actions have objectives which are realistic and fair. They take appropriate action without denying others.

Non-Verbal Cues

The body language of an aggressive person is replete with finger pointing, frowns, glares, stares, and rigid postures. His tone is critical and loud. A passive person has a submissive body language and his tone is low and lacks pitch variations. He nods head often and casts eyes down. An assertive person is attentive, interested and displays open gestures, direct eye contact, and a confident relaxed posture. His vocal volume is neither low nor high.

Verbal Cues

The vocabulary of an aggressive person consists of 'have tos,' 'oughts' and 'musts'. You will often find him speaking phrases like 'just do as I say,' or 'why don't you just do what I tell you to.' His language might be abusive. A passive person speaks fast when anxious and slows when in doubt. An assertive person will often use phrases like, 'I chose to,' 'I want more options,' and 'Is there another way.'

Feelings

Emotions of anger and hostility dominate an aggressive individual. But a passive individual is dominated by feeling of powerlessness and wonders why good work does not get duly rewarded. An assertive person is enthusiastic and even tempered.

Effects

When an aggressive person talks he provokes counter aggression, creates inharmonious environment, and wastes time and energy on supervising others. A passive person builds up dependency on relationships and promotes other's causes. An assertive individual works for himself as well as works for other causes he believes in.

Teams need members with assertive behavior. They want that their team members should kill the laziness which passivity brings and trash the aggression with involvement begets. This is called the art of balancing. You have to balance development and dominance, the ability to lead and to be led, to follow and to be followed, to guide and to be guided, to be creative and to pursue other to be creative, to take decisions and to abide by them.

A man walking a tightrope

8

DISPLAY AWARENESS AND CREATIVITY

Awareness

Topics given in a GD are usually general in nature so that they provide a level playing field to every participant. They are generally not chosen according to academic background of the participants.

Just speaking more in a GD can't take you too far. It is what you say that matters. If you speak much but say nothing you won't be able to crack the GD. So the very next question that will come in your mind is that how can you say more. Well, it requires a good ken, in depth knowledge of various aspects of our environment.

'Knowledge is power', is so much true when it comes to excelling at a GD. Sound knowledge in areas like politics, finance, economy, science, and technology is helpful but cannot be generated overnight. A candidate with consistent study habits has more chance of success.

To develop a sound knowledge base you must subscribe to at least one general knowledge magazine and to a few YouTube channels which are dedicated to giving you such info. Further, documentaries and TV channels like Discovery, History and National Geographic are a must to watch. Do not restrict yourself to watching only what you like. Explore new areas of information. Also, talk to people who have a wider ken and notice their approach while discussing a topic.

Creative Problem-Solving Skills

GD gives you a chance to generate and share new and innovative ideas. If you can come up with something creative you can gain a tremendous advantage. It would demonstrate your originality. Just make sure it is relevant to the topic.

Even in an interview, you may be asked to give examples of times you've demonstrated your creative problem-solving ability. It helps the interviewer to understand to how to think, learn how you address challenging situations and clarify how you can bring value to their organization.

In order to develop your creative problem-solving skills you need to first question the standard practices. When you question standard ways in which things are being done only then you open your mind towards what else is possible and how can it be better.

The next step is to relax your assumptions as they stop you from thinking beyond the boundaries. Besides, the boundaries you think exist may have in reality become obsolete by some technological advancement or might have been put wrongly in the first place. When you climb higher you can see farther. What appeared a limitation before may simply cease to exist now. This will help to search for unique innovative solutions for your current problem.

Finally practice empathy. Empathy is the ability to see your solution from the perspective of other people. If it is ultimately for the benefit of the team you don't want it to appear against their interests. Being empathetic will help you to tailor your solution to a people-friendly version before presenting it.

9

WAYS TO WIN ARGUMENTS

The ability to assert yourself is definitely one of the more valuable talents as assertiveness is required often in business and personal relationships. In a GD some of the other participants are going to oppose your position. Will you forcefully defend yourself in such a scenario? Or will you bide by your time, cornering the attacker later on?

There are times when the attacker has thrown in a silly point which you can let slide away. However, in case he has scored a knockdown you have to respond to safeguard your position.

You don't have to engage them in a war. Instead try to disarm them. Many times an elegant sentence is all you need to diffuse the situation. Here are some clever ways to communicate your position without bullying or offending other participants:

I understand your concern

This makes you appear sympathetic and comes off easy on the ears of the attacker. You position yourself as an ally rather than as an adversary. It also sounds sweet to the other present at the GD. So next time if you find someone opposing your views just use these words to diffuse him.

I agree, but

This is a gentle way to disarm your opponent. I call it 'the butt technique'. All is well till the point you say, 'I agree.' However, when you use the 'but' the story line changes altogether. It conveys that you have accepted the argument of the other side, when what you have actually done is nothing more than acknowledge it.

Poke fun at yourself before they do

Making fun of yourself is least offensive and least obvious ay of asserting yourself. However, once you make fun of yourself, it makes no sense for your opponents to do it anymore. You can say something like, 'I may be drifting a little here and wishing for stars as if I were a child, however, there is not harm in aiming for the stars.'

Blame it on something (not someone)

Sometimes to diffuse a potentially dangerous altercation it is important to depersonalize the issue. For instance, you may say that the weather is really hot and the sunlight coming from the window is perhaps getting to the adversary who is otherwise such a gentleman.

10

DEAL WITH DIFFICULT SITUATIONS

Things do not always turn out to be as we planned. The famous Murphy's Law, 'Anything that can go wrong will go wrong,' says it all. You have to be prepared to deal with any eventuality that may arise. Here are a few situations which may throw you off balance along with clever ways to deal with them:

Topic isn't Clear

If we do not clearly understand the meaning of the topic, do not ask the moderator for an explanation. Instead of displaying your ignorance in this manner, it is better to wait for some other participant to start to discuss the topic. So listen to the discussion carefully for the first few minutes and then when you have figured out what the topic is about start participating in the discussion.

Somebody Preempts You

If someone has already said what you wanted to speak, you have two choices.

1. Agree with the point made by that person and add on to it by displaying the applicability of the argument to different situations. By doing this, you will have broadened the scope of the argument.

2. Drop the point and think of fresh points.

To avoid getting into such a situation again, speak up in the first 4 to 5 minutes of the GD. If you wait longer, it is almost inevitable that someone will speak what you have in mind and probably take the job which you had in your dreams! Don't let that happen.

There is High Noise

It is difficult to participate when the noise level is too high. In such a scenario, you could try the following strategy. Identify the most powerful speaker in the group and note down the points that he is making. The moment the noise reduces a little, enter supporting the powerful speaker. You will have made a strong ally who will carry you through the noise.

English Not Fluent

Most of the GDs use English as a language for communication. Good command over English is certainly advantageous but will not compensate for lack of good content. If your content is good then even if your English might not be great, you must speak it out, rather than be inhibited by lack of good English. You will get credit for soundness of ideas.

Also, you can adopt roles which do not need you to speak longer sentences. You can support the idea presented by someone else and even invite the other reticent participants to offer their suggestions.

Aggressive Participant

You could use any of the following methods to deal with an aggressive participant:

- Ignore him and address the other members of the group.

- Be assertive and tell him that his argument is faulty.

- Point out to him that his point is well taken and that the group must progress further by discussing the ideas presented by others.

III
PART

POPULAR GD TOPICS

11

FACTUAL TOPICS

The environment shapes the lives of people and in return is also shaped by the actions of people. Factual topics are environment-related topics which test your awareness about the surroundings in which you live. These may include history and changes in geo-political arena, economic affairs and even the ecological habitat.

The moderators and judges expect that the candidates keep up with the recent happenings in the world and are able to relate the effect of those happenings to their everyday lives. Some of the factual topics which can be asked in a GD are given ahead.

- 'Gender Equality' in the workplace

- 'America First' Policy: Good or bad for World Geopolitics?

- Affordable healthcare in your country
- Age and youth: experience and young talent
- Are big dams necessary?
- Are celebrities treated unfairly by media?
- Are leaders born or made?
- Are we serious about saving wildlife and environment?
- Artificial intelligence–Pros and Cons
- Bad bank–Is it a good idea?
- Balance between profession and family
- Ban on Chinese Apps
- Bifurcation of Jammu & Kashmir
- BIMSTEC
- Blockchain Technology–Pros & Cons
- Brexit–Impact on EU?
- BRICS
- Can 'artificial intelligence' replace 'human intelligence'?
- Can 'death penalty' deter child rapes?
- Can celebrities make good politicians?
- Censorship of web series–Pros & Cons
- Challenges in the IT industry
- Child labour
- Child marriages
- China–Russia relations

- Circular economy is the key to sustainable development
- City vs. Village
- Climate Change–What can we do about it?
- Coaching centers are destroying education
- Commercialization of health care
- Compulsory yoga in schools–Pros and Cons
- Consumerism and middle class
- Controversy as a marketing strategy
- Corporate Social Responsibility–charity or marketing gimmick?
- Corruption in your country
- CPEC
- Criminalization of politics
- Cybercrime–A big challenge
- Data is the new oil
- Data Localisation–Benefits & Challenges
- Democracy vs. Monarchy
- Detention policy–Pros & Cons
- Digital Revolution–Pros & Cons
- Disaster Management in our country
- Do brands rule our lives?
- Does 'NOTA' option in elections really make sense?
- Does corporate world promote entrepreneurship?
- Does UNSC need to be reformed?

- Drug menace–How to fight with it?
- E-Commerce–Sustainable business model?
- Effects of video games on well-being
- E-learning–Pros & Challenges
- Electric vehicles
- End of globalization
- Ethical manager vs. Effective manager
- Ethics in Politics–Myth or Reality?
- Ever growing air pollution levels–Where does the problem lie?
- EVMs vs. Paper Ballots
- E-waste management
- Facebook–Cambridge Analytica data scandal
- Facebook vs. LinkedIn
- Factors that contributed to the growth of MNCs
- Fake News–Impact on society
- Fixed pay vs. Variable pay
- Free WiFi Spots–Beneficial or not?
- Freebie politics in India
- Freedom of Press in your country
- G20
- Generation Gap
- Green jobs are essential for sustainable development
- Hard Work vs. Smart Work

- Higher education in our country
- How can slums be improved?
- How can the standard of people below the poverty line be raised?
- How can tourism be improved?
- How can we deal with increasing cyber crimes?
- How can we reduce wealth gap between rich & poor?
- How can we stop 'honor killings'?
- How can we utilize technology to tackle financial crimes?
- How to create more jobs in rural areas?
- How to deal with international terrorism?
- How to eliminate the threat of nuclear war?
- How to reduce NPA?
- How to solve the issue of pending cases in courts
- If Third World War happens, what will be the possible reason behind it?
- Impact of COVID-19 on environment
- Impact of COVID-19 on global economy
- Impact of demonetization on Indian Economy
- Impact of movies on youth
- Impact of news channels on society
- Impact of technology on banking sector
- Impact of technology on jobs
- Impact of US withdrawal from Iran nuclear deal

- In what way 'Payment Banks' are useful?
- India–Pakistan relations
- India-US relations
- Indiscriminate tourism will lead to environmental damage
- Industrial Revolution
- Information overload
- Insolvency and bankruptcy code
- Interlinking of rivers–Pros & Cons
- Is advertising beneficial or not?
- Is educational qualification necessary for politicians?
- Is globalization a threat to cultural heritage of a country?
- Is internet curbing creativity?
- Is it really worth to become a cashless economy?
- Is nuclear disarmament mandatory to achieve 'world peace'?
- Is stock market similar to gambling?
- Is technology creating income inequalities?
- Is technology making us less human?
- Is the concept of non-violence still applicable?
- Is the world ready for 'electric cars'?
- Is there a need to curb the mushrooming of private coaching institutes?
- Is war the best way to solve international disputes?

- Is your country prepared enough to handle cyber attacks?
- Job vs. Entrepreneurship
- Joint family vs. Nuclear family
- Knowledge based economy is important to achieve the economic boom
- Lessons for the world from COVID-19 pandemic
- Light pollution–A new threat
- Live-in relationships
- Love marriage vs. Arranged marriage
- Manager vs. Leader
- Maritime security of the world
- Markets are found not created
- Mechanisms adopted to combat terrorism
- Mental illness in your country
- Mixed gender education–Pros & Cons
- Mob lynchings in your country
- Mobile towers in residential areas–harmful or not?
- Modernisation of armed forces
- Modi's Prime Ministership–Impact on the world
- Modi's Prime Ministership–Pros & Cons
- Movies encourage social evils
- National Education Policy
- National Health ID–Pros, Cons & Challenges
- National Recruitment Agency–Pros & Challenges

- National Register of Citizens–merits & demerits
- Nationalism vs Regionalism
- Net neutrality
- Nuclear energy–boon or bane?
- Nuclear waste management
- Open Book Exams–Pros, Cons & Challenges
- Parliamentary System vs. Presidential System
- Plastic ban: Economy vs. Environment
- Plastic Money–Merits & Demerits
- Plastic Pollution
- Population explosion–boon or bane?
- Print Media vs Digital Media
- Privatization will lead to less corruption
- Public perception of the police–How can it be improved?
- Recapitalization of Banks
- Referendums strengthen democracy
- Relevance of Gandhi in modern world
- Relevance of WTO in today's global scenario
- Retirement Homes–Pros & Cons
- Right to be forgotten
- Right to Education: Success or Failure?
- Rise and fall of communism
- Rising stress levels
- Role of engineers in disaster management

- Role of ethics in business
- Role of UN in peace keeping
- Role of women be in combat situations
- Role of your country in United Nations
- Should 'physical education' be made compulsory in schools?
- Should agricultural subsidies be stopped?
- Should artistic expression be monitored by law?
- Should Marijuana be legalized?
- Should Non-IT students be allowed for IT jobs?
- Should public sector banks be privatized?
- Significance of BRICS in world economy
- Social Media–Impact on human behavior and society
- Statue of Liberty
- Statue of Unity
- Status of sports in your country
- Status of women in your country
- Student suicides–What are the deep-rooted problems?
- Surrogacy
- Syrian crisis
- Technocrats should not become bureaucrats
- Technology changing the face of education
- The future of crypto currencies
- The menace of eve-teasing

- The menace of trolling
- The New Farm Bill–Pros, Cons & Challenges
- Traffic problems in your country
- Trial by Media–Pros and Cons
- Triple Talaq Law
- Turkey-France Relations
- Unemployment Allowance–Pros & Cons
- Unemployment scenario in your country
- Unique identification number for every citizen
- Universal Basic Income–Pros & Cons
- Urbanisation
- USA–Iran relations
- US-China Trade war–Impact on USA, China & other countries
- Use of renewable energy in your country
- US-Mexico border wall–Good or Bad?
- Water scarcity in your country
- What can we do to eradicate poverty?
- What is the biggest problem that India is facing?
- Which one is more important–creativity or knowledge?
- Why is molestation prevalent in your country?
- Why is Norway the world's happiest country?
- Will artificial intelligence take away jobs?
- Work from home–Pros & Cons

- Youth empowerment is necessary for any country's development
- Zero Budget Natural Farming

12

CONTROVERSIAL TOPICS

Controversial topics are issues which do not have a clearly defined 'yes' or 'no' answers. There will be many people who are in support of the issue and many against it. So generally there will be nothing such as right or wrong. They are a matter of pure choice.

When controversial topics are given for discussion the moderators know that the chances of heated arguments are high. In giving such topics for discussion their intention is to assess your capability of how well you receive the divergent views and how successful you are in presenting your point of view. Your ability to think structurally and present convincingly is crucial when discussing controversial topics.

A list of controversial topics used for group discussions is given ahead:

- Aggressive vs. Passive—which parenting style is better?
- An eye for an eye: Is it a right policy?
- Are CCTV cameras in public places effective or just an invasion of privacy?
- Are corporate jobs a new form of slavery?
- Are men silent sufferers in this modern world?
- Are women better managers than men?
- Can 'world peace' be achieved?
- Can illiterates be given driving licenses?
- Can Temples have gender-specific rules?
- Can women be in combat roles?
- Cow Slaughter Ban—Right or wrong?
- Do deadlines destroy creativity?
- Do small companies have more harmony?
- Does 'universal adult franchise' needs to be reviewed?
- Does nepotism exist in Hollywood?
- Experimenting on Animals—Is it fair?
- FDI in retail—Boon or Bane?
- Freedom is a myth
- How far crypto currencies like Bitcoin can be relied upon?
- Innovation vs Invention—What is more important?
- Involving Army in civil tasks—Right or Wrong?
- Is censorship of movies an outdated concept?

- Is cricket an overrated sport in India?
- Is football an overrated sport in Brazil?
- Is human gene modification good for civilization?
- Is MBA a rat race?
- Is online piracy inevitable?
- Is our country becoming intolerant?
- Is our country safe for women?
- Is the United Nations still relevant?
- Is WikiLeaks a bane or a boon?
- MBAs do not make good business leaders
- MBAs do not make good business leaders
- Might is always right
- Money spent on space exploration can be better used on reducing poverty on earth
- News channels–breaking rules to give breaking news
- Reservation for economically weaker people– Good or Bad?
- Should 'Freedom of expression' have limits?
- Should 'Group Discussion' be compulsory in the hiring process?
- Should 'Right to Privacy' have limits?
- Should adultery be criminalized?
- Should alcohol consumption be banned?
- Should anonymity be allowed on the internet?
- Should attempt to suicide be decriminalized?

- Should beauty pageants be banned?
- Should betting and gambling be legalized?
- Should both developed and underdeveloped countries have equal binding in combating climate change?
- Should capital punishment be banned?
- Should Chinese products be banned?
- Should driverless cars be allowed in India?
- Should gay marriages be allowed?
- Should homeschooling be encouraged in India?
- Should homosexuality be legalized?
- Should India accept Rohingya refugees?
- Should killing of stray animals be legalized?
- Should marital rape be criminalized in India?
- Should military training be made compulsory for all?
- Should mobile phones be allowed in schools & colleges?
- Should organ donation be made compulsory?
- Should political parties be brought under RTI Act?
- Should politics and business be mixed?
- Should pornographic content be banned?
- Should rapists be tortured?
- Should reality shows be banned?
- Should reservations be based on economic status?
- Should smoking be banned?

- Should street food be banned?
- Should the internet be censored?
- Should the language spoken by majority be the National language?
- Should the rich and wealthy be taxed more?
- Should Triple Talaq be abolished?
- Should uniforms be mandatory in schools?
- Should women be encouraged to work in night shifts?
- The pen is mightier than the sword
- US-Mexico border wall–Good or Bad?
- Why is molestation prevalent in India?
- The world does not need religion
- Who serves the country most–teacher or solider?
- Should technocrats be allowed to head an organization?
- Should women be encouraged to work in night shifts?
- Should environment polluters be severely punished?
- Should there be a retirement age for politicians?
- Should mother tongue be the medium of instruction in schools?
- Should Fathers be given Paternity Leave?
- Is hosting Olympics good for the host country?
- Do business and ethics go hand in hand?

- Should attendance be made compulsory for students?
- Should betting and gambling be legalized in your country?
- Should zoos be abolished?
- Genetically modified products–Boon or bane?
- Multinational Companies: Are they devils in disguise?
- Should euthanasia/mercy killing be legalized?

13

ABSTRACT TOPICS

Abstract topics are not quite logical. Neither do they test your knowledge-base nor do they test your ability to present your arguments in a cogent manner. Abstract topics are meant to challenge your creative skills and provoke you to think out-of-the-box. A list of abstract topics used for group discussions is given ahead:

- Black or Grey
- Blood is thicker than water
- Blue is better than red
- Door
- Dot
- Famous or important
- Important or nice

- Money is honey
- Money is sweeter than honey
- Pink
- Red
- Roots & wings
- Walls are dead
- Zero

UNTIL WE MEET AGAIN

The ability to join in discussion and ask questions is essential in higher studies as well in modern job environment. In case you have trouble with speaking or asking questions in study classes you may try the following strategies:

1. **Observe**: Start attending seminars and workshops and notice what other participants do. Focus on how do they ask questions, make critical comments and agree or disagree with arguments. Pay attention to the language they use while tactfully showing their disagreement and the gestures they use when they want to interrupt or make a pint.

2. **Practice**: Invite a few friends and start discussing a topic of common interest. Ask them for their opinion, try to voice your disagreements politely and choose different roles at different times.

3. **Participate**: Start taking active part in informal and formal discussions. While participating do make sure that you contribute in some or the other way.

During the discussion, prepare a question to ask, or agree with another speaker's remarks.

Demands and styles of the job market place continually change, This book is based on real GDs rather than theory. Your experience in the job market as a GD participant (or moderator) would be helpful. Your comments and suggestions make my day.

Reach me at: drprabalfranknandwani@gmail.com.

ACKNOWLEDGEMENTS

I am grateful to all the universities and colleges who entrusted me with the task of preparing their students for group discussions. It gave me an opportunity to study about GDs, practically conduct GDs, note the shortcomings of the candidates and device strategies to overcome those shortcomings.

I am also grateful to my students who not only participated with me also encouraged me to write a book on this important step of the recruitment process.

ABOUT
THE SKILLS ACADEMY

We are small team of experts who specialize in things to do with helping people to be more successful in their careers–guidance, advice, coaching, mentoring, assisting individuals with their CVs and even grooming them from interviews.

We work with organisations providing consultancy on devising career development systems on the people side of mergers, acquisitions and downsizing particularly in the area of outplacement. We also work with individuals from chair person to tea person helping them to become the very best they can.

It does not matter if you represent a large organisation or a single individual working on your own, if you would like assistance from us just contact us at theskillsacademy@gmail.com. To know more about us logon to www.theskillsacademy.net.

We look forward to the opportunity of working with you because your success will be our success.

Job Related Services

1. Professional Resume Creation
2. Grooming for Interviews
3. Mock Interview Session
4. Mock GD Session